S0-BND-938

The Troubled House

SHEILA O'HAGAN

The Troubled House

SALMON POETRY

Published in 1995 by
Salmon Publishing Ltd,
Upper Fairhill, Galway

© Sheila O'Hagan 1995

The moral right of the author has been asserted.

A catalogue record for this book is available from the British Library.

ISBN 1 897648 16 2

Cover illustration by Conor Hutchinson
Back cover photograph by Steve Humphreys
Cover design by Poolbeg Group Services Ltd
Set by Poolbeg Group Services Ltd in Goudy 11/13
Printed by Colour Books, Baldoyle Industrial Estate, Dublin 13.

For Dermot

Acknowledgements

The author is grateful to the editors of the following publications in which many of these poems first appeared:

Acorn, Cobwebs, The Connacht Tribune, Cyphers, Force 10, Fortnight, Irish Studies Review, The Leinster Leader, Lines Review, The Observer, Poetry Australia, Poetry Ireland Review, Windows.

Also acknowledged: 'Ireland's Women' – Anthology, edited by Katie Donovan, A. Norman Jeffares and Brendan Kennelly.

The author is thankful for support provided by the Arts Council through the Arts Council – Aer Lingus Travel Awards program.

SALMON PUBLISHING LIMITED

receives financial assistance from the

Arts Council/An Chomhairle Ealaíon.

.

Contents

The Unborn

Trying to unmake myself I take a journey
Through closed eyes to a garden shady
With stirrings, plucks of wind continuous
As harps, air pink as sherbet

All the Unborn in a thready line
A golden dog coddling them along
While disembodied voices sing
The loveliness of the unplumbed

And beyond the garden, shudders,
Glad cries, a nearby ping
As each blithe spec takes off
Whizzing to its beginning

Before me stands an angel, wings at ease
Haven't you been here before she says –
I edge into a grotto, hide my face
Until her shadow's passed

Find that she has put an apple
In my hand. Falling through mothy cloud
I catch up with the Unborn all starry eyed
Wait, it's not all good, I say. Sometimes . . .

I Dream My Mother

For instance, in this dream
two trees – a copperbeach,
a lilac shining like a ballroom

Are you, dolorous leaves
of the beech obscuring
the lilac of your youth

That bobs a frock of white
as if to girlish music
as I run to free you, loosen

Your copperheavy hair,
place on the gramophone
a dance for your bright shoes

But you are gone
and then I see
that I am also beech and lilac tree.

The Fur Coat

She sits alone in church
Her mother gone away,
A fur coat dozes
On the seat beside her.
She wants to sink her hands
Into its lushy depths
But her hands are tight in prayer
As she's been taught.

She prays her mother
Will come home and grow
A coat all over so her little girl
Is never cold again.
The fur coat stirs,
She smells the mother smell,
Her insides hurt,
Soon she will be five.

Hail Holy Queen she prays
Give us this day
Thy blessing and thy grace.
Inside the pocket of the coat
Her mother plays with dolls.

The Garden at 4 am

It is when she steps into the rose garden
the show starts. Having nowhere to go
she is compelled to go there,

Learns to abandon her limbs to the music,
reedy, legato. In her sea of desire
drowns quickly. Sighs engulf her.

By the fountain she rests, sonorous plash plash,
latice gates opening and shutting, but he is not
under the something tree, not in the nest

Of the snowy bird, and she has scoured
the house, empty, chattering. He is not himself
she says, he is not himself at all.

Water Woman

This supine nude I stare on,
Myself in bath. Bonnard
Wants to paint me, legs
Of Dordogne green, asymmetric
Hips, all still.

Go away, Bonnard,
I'm no fish woman
To be slabbed in strict form.
I'll paint myself
Squidge fingers in the soap
To join up stipple moles,
Trace the inbetween
And undulating
Inlet of the legs,
Bays of the underarm.

And my waterlily breasts,
With what brushwave do I cup
Your pink convex, caress
That arch of rhomboid thigh.

Light moving in the water,
Water moving in the light.
This is no still life.
See how the rounded plane
Of my blue belly
Is now dappled
Now doused in yellow
From the swinging bulb
That catching my thicket,
Glints the way
To the rosemadder pool.

Now I see me in reverse,
My underwater shade.
When I let the water out
One of me
Will slip away
Leaving behind
A beryl green
Soul rim
For you, Mr Bonnard.

The Red Shoes

They were that big. Stilts,
swaggered me all over town.
I was taller than any man,
my clicks and clacks

a one woman red brigade.
Power surged through my toes,
my heels, my legs, office doors
swung open.

They're still alive, those shoes.
My daughter, man-eater Niamh,
set up her easel yesterday,
painted them by a hat of green.

Late Spring in Stephen's Green

I want to say
Damn the winter
Endless whinge of wind
And sullen days
When suddenly colour again
The sky hangs aquamarine
Youth swings on the limbs of trees

And I rush out to meet the sun
My eyes mad with patterns
Of flowers and things –
Flounce of the cherry
Heavy with child,
Moved by a bit of a breeze
The lush and sway of the limes,
Paddle happy ducks
Crisscrossing the pond
With dribbles of chicks.

Over and over this born again act
Fools me into a new beginning
As I say to myself
Yes.

Aubade

Is it the senses or the soul knows best?
The early day, curve of a road on which
Light moves like a painter's brush, violet
Fall of mountains to the sea, a sea-sent wind
To sway the barley fields, notes from a bird's
Throat wild enough to lift me from the known.

Such is the way the day shakes out her mood,
Breathes on the earth, arranges herself
In storm and pastoral. Capricious
And lovely bitch, she leads me to think
The senses move in heaven, not the soul.

Yellow Bird

A yellow bird
flies into
the web of my eyes

Slits my dark
like the streak at the heart
of the iris

As if my mind
were a door left ajar
for every rushing thing

It is the flame
that makes its mark
out of nothing

Soon it will be
a brazen tiger
who stalks my space

Its yellow stripes
staring through
black bars

Undine

Inside me is Lethean,
a river's shale
of muddied whispers,
my mouth a river bank
that strains for the shapes
I have been waiting for.

Against my tongue
old sounds lap slack,
shallows tell themselves
in rings of brown

And I search the waters
for new springs,
chase stringy light
to find news of sacred places,
words under stones.

Suddenly my throat
where the river rises
is a sybil's
As I break out of myself
casting my song
from dark rockpools.

Muse

When I see a fixed star
shift one millimetre –
hold it, you say, that pin's glint
may be your diamond absolute.

Or, eyes closed, aspire to see
Keats' flowers, Kavanagh's fields,
passing a ditch, catch
the flame of a wildflower, single and mute,
any prick of form striving to be itself,
your voice insists:

> *Grasp, cling*
> *as if to a trout in water,*
> *elusive, silvered.*

The Return of Odysseus to Ithaca

When he limped home smelling of the world, stood under
The great gate of the courtyard, shreds of vigour
In the wiry hair, the ageing limbs still sinewed
She saw him from her window, knew she had acted right
But hard with anger for the loveless wait, withdrew
Into the shadows of her room, for three days cried
To her unborn sons, counted twenty notches
On the olive post he'd hewn and whittled for their bed
Heard his bellowed rage from the old banquet hall
Swagger of the warrior his gander up, thud of crossbolt
Cudgelled skulls, blood on the tapestries, and when
His anger spent, he leant exhausted by the fireplace
She fixed her face and hair, came down to him, cradled
His fading manhood and drew the sting of their lost years.

Orpheus and Eurydice

When Orpheus sings the houses shake
The baby's fat feet twitch,
On the third floor old Pluto's whore complains,
A thousand townbirds pass the word around
Cars squeal, horns blare, my hands linger
On his rastafarian hair.

But when he goes into the streets
I'm left in this dark house
With cooking, children, and the upstairs whore.
One day I'll leave the baby with that sour bitch
And follow Orpheus till he looks around
And says 'Woman, go home.'

Sisyphus

She pushes up and down the hill from home
To supermarket with the babykart,
The bag of wash, the toys for the park.
In a month the new baby will come,
The wash grow bigger and the little lad
Run off up and down the shopping aisles.
She stops to draw a hand across her back,
Light up a fag, count out her life in child
Allowance days. Tomorrow she will trail
Round to the clinic, have her stomach probed,
Her urine tested, get weighed and be told
He should do some voluntary, not be home
So much. She doesn't answer them. Sometimes
She paints her face and goes out with the girls.

Antigone

There is no light. She breathes slowly,
Allows herself an hour for dreaming –
Of spring in Thebes, wildflowers barbarous
On the hills, air tumbling between
Her thighs, her arms, her smallest bones.
By starlight she had crept from Argos
To track her bad boy brother, used
Hands and nails to claw earth for his grave,
Knew that like the last bright star
She would disappear before morning.

Walled in stone, her time has come.
She spits the dark out of her mouth
And with a cry of the thing done,
Defiance becomes myth, her soul
Fills the space of that sentinel star
To lamplight all the nights when a sister
Creeps along the pitted road to lay a coat
Over the riven body of her brother.

Watercolour

A perfect day, sun enough, blown cloud,
The stippled trees, their caught light
Doubled in the lake, the chasing brush.

As if I'd marked it wrong, a shower,
And images dissolve, runnels of colour
Down the page, outlines of tree and lake

Fade into shimmering. Something brims here,
Taps into other, overlay of light and leaf
And watery rush numinous as cinema

The brush splays to catch.
But on a drying page the painting
With the rainstorm slips away.

Looking into Corot's 'Ville d'Avray'

Corot is my winter laureate,
Draws me from the cold into the gallery
To wander among river, field and tree
Ether white beneath a sluggard sky,
A figure turning from the riverbank
To look at me, and overall the drift
Of an uncanny mist so though I know
Where tree, field and riverbank should be,
Each is wraithlike, silvered, vapourised

As if this were the last landscape
The gods had visited in stealth,
Laid down a cloth of shadeless light,
And the riverbank recedes, the trees
give up their skeletal identity,
The girl figure has already crossed
The river and is waiting for me.

Seurat's Gray Weather Dots

One of those diaries, a painting for each month.
I open November – Gray Weather: Grande Jatte
as seen by Seurat from the island shore,
staid riverway, motionless boats, trees bent

in the stillness peculiar to winter,
his Sunday people all gone home. And yet
this painting sings although a gray day
was the intent, a rendered dot by dot

to batten down the sway towards light,
each dot so neatly placed, so pointaliste,
but underneath the unifying gray
a scintillation as if, at a touch

of sun, the boats might blow yellow smoke,
take off, birds burst from trees, the leaves
pulse blue and green, the roofs squint pink.
In a painter's eye no gray exists.

Taking Lily to the Tate

When Lily was two
I took her to the Tate,
in the sculpture hall
let her go her way

Saw her draw near
a woman full of augeries,
her head turned inside out
like a seethrough bird.

Lily tried to climb
into the caverns of her mind
but intimidated by her stillness

Found a mother shape
perfectly round
and more accessible

And another bird
of sold gold
a Maiastra
singing to an emperor
who inspired her

So she ran into the picture gallery,
on the wall
saw a large coloured spider
with square feet
unfolding itself slowly
from a sandbag

And with wonderful invention
she made her own spiral
dancing in and out, out and in –
I thought of a bee against a windowframe –

After this celebration
she came across
some desert flowers
so red they made her eyes revolve

And rested beside them
maybe hoping to absorb their red
but she could only manage pink
so in a little huff
she moved on and came to

A curious singing lesson
hanging in a corner,
tried to read
its joined up lines and circles,
made all sorts of up and down sounds
ending on a squeaky C

Then very tired
found the Rothko room
in all that dark maroon
remembered how it was
to nestle in a womb
(or so it seemed)
for she fell asleep.

Cubist Bash

Rumseeped the letters tell of téte-a-tétes
Or conversations from Le Figaro
The dancing demoiselles trip through the silt
Of strings and music sheets drifty as snow

As Ma Jolie her tinkleglass uptilts
To toast the deconstructed violin
Ah la petite chanson the leitmotif
All liquidlimp and aphrodesian

Fishflat the palette cools to silvergreen
In sepia tones the fluted shadows drone
O happypink o spotted sugarcube
And clinka clink of absintheslippy spoon

The brillig drinkledrops of les amis –
George Braque and Pablo P are making whoopee

Anne Devlin
(1780-1851)

i Croneybeag

It was powerful in Wicklow
that spring, whitethorn
sprawled on roads, wildflowers

Gone mad, the crows
thrown black against the sky.
God how I loved to run

The lanes of Croneybeag, jump
the streams, my hair in my face,
fearless in my limbs

As I hid oatmeal in the earth
for those men, twelve or thereabouts,
cousins Hugh, Pat and Art

Would be hiding out in the best
and worst of weathers
on Wicklow brakes and bogs.

I was one of them, Anne Devlin,
runner for the cause,
my head full of death and love.

ii My Father's House

Devlin, a rebel name, though
my father's house is safe
until the day a strange woman

Comes across the door, looks around
as if she's lost her way,
sees a man in a woman's apron

Stand to churn – the tale she tells,
she an informer's wife.
That day the luck is turned,

I am taken to a Mr Emmet's house
in Butterfield Lane, to act as
housekeeper and go-between.

This is young Anne, my father says,
You may place the lives
of thousands in her hands.

iii Mr Emmet

Such work to do,
the house is paper strewn,
messengers come and go.

Under timber for the pikes
I pack powder and ball,
cocked hats and uniforms,

Keep count of all who's out
and all who's in, of monies
spent, food got, keep from him

All but his nearest men.
There is meeting after meeting
then the bad night come,

Panic, a false alarm, confusion
in the city, dead soldiers, our own
scattered. Some return.

Bad cess to you, I scream,
have you destroyed the kingdom?
Where are my kin?

Mr Emmet, he was that full
of anxiety, yet as he left with them
took my hands, looked at me

In such a manner I cannot forget.
Goodbye Anne, he said,
Keep trust for us.

iv The Arrest

Never in my father's house
heard I a bad word said.
The words them soldiers use

Pain me more deep than
the bayonets that puck my breasts,
obscenities fouling my womanhood,

My decency mocked, foul lies even as I
deny all they say, my young sister
looking on, pertrified, she too

Covered in blood where their bayonets
have pucked her. She is eight.
Then when they are done

With their play, they swing me off
a cart . . . merciful god, my breath cut
I plunge through time and dark

Into that Presence, who wears
all stilly radiant Mr Emmet's face.
Cut down and breathing still,

From that moment my deep self transformed,
I'm taken to the hated name and place,
Royal Jail, Kilmainham.

v The Cell

Cold blankets me, I crawl
against the wall, my shift so damp
it leaves a trail of slime.

A year in this hole, length of a bed,
knife chill, wind whip, floor of stone,
the black door through which you come,

Dr Trevor, Governor's tool, harrower
of men and women, I tell you
I know naught of heroism

Save in the set of a word.
So though you do for me, your venom,
your foul tongue, it is I who

Day after day, throw that last
bitter word to shore with pride
my unbending soul.

I retch from my own smell
but were your soul exposed
the stench would empty hell.

vi The Execution

Who crouches in the corner. Is it he?
Come here, dear Sir, and lay your head
on Annie's knee.

In a covered cart they take me out
to see where pigs drink your blood
in Thomas Street.

For three year and a half I will endure
the murderous cold of this hole
without blanket or cot

Day after day in such loneliness
of heart and spirit, beg God for help
to hold onto some sense in my head

And in the unchanging dark
of night and day, I learn to call up
on the wall the icon of your face

Sometimes hear voices form the fields
call me to Croneybeag, but who would know
my swollen legs, my cratered skin

Crabs in my half closed eyes,
and who would save my love
from burial in Bully's Field.

vii My Release

In a half-dead state,
near blind, lame, my health gone,
they let me go

To forty year of poverty, the scourge.
I walk the streets, my only rest
a hovel in the Coombe

Without water, scarce any food,
wash in the Dodder – oh the green trees
that do lean over me, the soft grass underfoot.

I'll die soon for none come near.
Who is the man who passes me with lowered head?
I hear informers' whispers from the cells.

A bell rings. Annie is leaving you.
Burn a light for her in Number Two,
Little Elbow Lane, the Coombe.

The Troubled House

The purpose of poetry is to remind us how difficult it is to remain just one person, for our house is open, there are no keys in the doors, and invisible guests come in and out at will.
— Czeslaw Milosz

I live in a troubled house,
walk backwards, stumble over things,
a piano tinkers, the fretting wind
cannot find a tune, eyes dark as anemones
follow me from room to room,
along the corridor shuffle of empty shoes,
petitioners, their hands held out for love.
My dears, you cannot live with me,
the moment's passed, having no breath
you exhale loss. Besides it is my guilt
excites you, another country where you died.
I want to say to you yes come tonight
from three to four, I'll leave the door ajar
but do not stay. Let silence settle
like an old dog on the floor. This house
must decompose. At daybreak I'll close it down,
go into the garden, wait for snow
to spread in absolution.

The Wood Pigeon

A tree bends over you like Yeats' old thorn,
How desolate the day, your place in it.
I push the graveyard gate, walk slowly through
The gloomy avenues of fern and stone.
I buried you in the wrong place, the wind
Is softer from the west then from the east,
Your feet should face the sea like any Celt.
But I'll do what I can to clear your space,
Brush off the sodden leaves, replace the lead
Of letters fallen off your name, our name.
And I'll not ask what of you perished first
Yet hear the truth, that all is gathered up
In human love. I've left you some flowers.
Is it the rain or you who flays my face,
Or wind dements my hair? I turn to leave,
A wood pigeon breaks from the trees, a whirr
Soft as a ghost. I listen to it
As it comes and goes, comes and goes.

Night Air

I love your walking in on me each night,
Not the usual wisp and tatter
Of the undressed ghost but resolute
And bright in your own clothes,
Outstretched hands saying it is I.

But come and see, outside this room
The salvias still bloom, the window breathes
Warm air through rattan slats, in the French door
Shines the bronze haze of the crysanthemums,
Strange you are not reflected there.

Needing no space you are in me, light seeps
Down your sleeves, out of your shoes. Sit down,
Your glass is filled, have you seen Schubert?
I thought my heart tomb dark and cold
But love is rogue and it is I who call you.

Where You Are

I know the country you are in
is near. Around me linger whispers,
a supernal scent, and the way
you once put your hand on my head
happens again and again.

I know your eyes will still be sad,
your hands inclined to wring themselves
into solutions. I couldn't hold you back
nor follow you into dark.

But I say to you this night,
whatever you feel or hear or see
tell me; whatever country you are in,
be there for me, all mother bright
and welcoming.

Elegy for Mark

In the stored past of an attic
I, a woman growing old,
Hold a coat, Oxfam with rabbit pin
That shapes the lie of your presence,
Arrange the sleeves in an embrace,
Search for a familiar hair, a stain
Mourning as older women do
The bodies of the young,

Watch how your shade invades the pool
Of sun the window has let in,
Hear the purr of the Silver Dream
Racer along a country road,
See it turn treacherous
as you bend to the fatal spin,
The reflection of your stillness
In the still turning wheels.

I, a woman growing old,
Perform a ritual for another's son
Loved as my own, rock myself
Into a grief black as the coat
I hold lest you be there, once a year
Climbing the height of this house
Far from any who might hear
The beat of the heart mending.

Are You Lonesome Tonight

Taking up the doorway
Of the Pizza Hut
You pour sweetlipped songs
Into a beercan microphone,
My Brixton Elvis
Gone inside your head
To hold onto a good time.

Twenty years on
Rock and roll hips,
Windmill limbs
Sway the same numbers
To squad car trumpets,
Ambulance saxophones,
One of the unhappy happy
Who live in public doors.

I clap hands for your song –
(*Are You Lonesome Tonight*,
Heartbreak Hotel) –
As I wait for a bus
That doesn't come,
Remember a time when I wore
Tinsel at Christmas
For extra razzmatazz.

Aisling

Inside his Asti Spumante box
Donated by Jacksons of the Strand
(Who didn't say they don't employ blacks)
Double cluster bubbles overhead
Were Marilyn Carol Sharon Jan
And he Actaeon limp in a Porsche.

A View form Mars

In the photograph, a god face
Stares from his shadowy head
In monolithic pose, the raddled eyes
Telling he holds vigil for his tribes
Cocooned in ice, their faces glazed,
Their warrior bones caught
In the haze of the old planet.

Gestating beneath those rose-lit layers
A master breed, bodies alabastered,
Voices trailed on filaments of wind
Thinner than sonic, as they wait
In the shimmer of his dreaming gaze
For Mars to warm, the ice
To bloom into resurrection.

Juxtapose the dreaming gaze
With the gaze of the red-hued ones
Across Nebraskan plains whose fathers,
Red Cloud, Geronimo, wait under ochre clay
For the second visitation –
Fiery avengers, shrill voiced priests
Come to school the new race.

Lazarus to his Sisters

In your house at Bethany
unable to love Him

I had looked at Him
with lascivious eyes

   (the toss and furl
   of magenta hair

   the carnal mouth
   the lissom thighs)

Was turned to stone
by the blow of denial

     *

Into the flame of morning
He hauled me

Trailing my linen
my soul's gossamer

For an instant I stood
tasting the miracle

As He opened my eyes
unwrapped my face

Melting the rock
of my grief

To ashes of flesh
glitter of blood

And I took shape
the lover redeemed

Clutched at redberries
staining the scorched

White of His robe
with stigmata

*

Later my sisters you said
it had been a rehearsal

The Student Astronomer

Years living high in a cave
He smells
Only the whizzy chemicals
Of the stars,
Bathes in their mild light
Blowing like smoke in his eyes.

Discovers his love
A bluebright quasar
Hanging like a prayer
Calls her Sylvia,
Meticulously charting
Her vagrant ways.

Requests the Faculty
to sit his examination
In celestial research
But no they say, no no
You may not sit with us
You smell of earth.

George Eliot and Raphael

Wandering in Dresden,
Has a bloc on 'Adam Bede',
Takes an apartment for fourteen days,
So capable, she worried

Would she ever finish.
On the second day went to the Gallery,
Sat before the Sistine Madonna –
Virgin and Child with St Barbara and St Anne
As seen by Raphael,

Each day of her stay
Absorbing his symmetry,
The way a curve found its opposite,
A tone its complement,
The movement of a hand or head
To find a partner and complete the move,
Every fold a runnel of colour
Making a music in itself,
And in Marianne,

Who returned to London
To finish Adam. Selling ever since,
It broke new ground in symmetry.
I wish she'd kept her name,
Marianne, so sinuous,
George, so crude.

Abduction

Three angels with navy wings
slip into my room, heads bent
in unison, looking for some ghost
or soul, with low coo's rest awhile
before they take off round the wall,
slip between Paul Henry's strange
and lovely mountains, by the window
where the desk grows, emerge
to hover meekly by the Raphael
Madonna who lowers her exquisite lids
in greeting, a sudden whoosh,
they're camped on the rosy shores
of Paul Gauguin's Tahiti, wing tips
a little damp, next stop the couch,
forest of peacocks and flowers,
into cushions out again, no clues
in those chintz thickets, I knew
what they were looking for, the forlorn
soul of Keats sleeping in the grate
lit by the warm moon of the standard lamp,
I'd carried his death mask all the way
from Rome, reading to him nightly
Seamus Heaney and Endymion.

With whoops and cries they find him,
cradle him within rococo wings,
his siren nightingales, eyes all moist,
rounded mouths all ooh's, dissolve beneath
the door, sliver of light, whiff of wind.
I fill the grate with flowers,
wipe away the scorch marks on the wall.

Swifts at Leonardo da Vinci Airport

In the dreaming lounge
Of the Leonardo da Vinci Airport
I sit out the evening
My plane unable
To choke up an air stream.

In and around the terminal
Swifts are reeling
With zig zag hysteria
Witch black against the light.

                    *

On a stone seat
Rosed in the sun
Of the Umbrian afternoon
He sits, covers a drawing sheet
With the bones of birds
Hollow, honeycombed, the swifts

Who shadow the run of his pen
Bowed wings, spilt tails
Playing spitfires between
Terracotta roofs
Shaded gables.

One falls on the ground
Its brown thinness
Shivers against cupped hands
A warm thumb probes
The fragile anatomy
Feels its need of an airstream.

He stretches his full length
To place it on the roof
A pause for balance
Then down it swoops
And up, and off.

*

Bathed in his own light
Leonardo moves into the mist
Of the screaming tail
As I board my plane

And I reach out to touch him
Who dreamed of man
Skittering on bony wings
Through lanes of air.

Michael's Fireflies

It was not
the utter turquoise of the sea
the goldspun sands
the jewel coves
that was his miracle

But, where he sat
in the dark softening
of the day's heat,
a flaming spancel of fireflies
round the lemon tree.

He called on me to look
and I saw the flares of his promise,
drop like dreams in the lap –
light splints on needle bones
bat of the eye in sleep.

Fireflies are everywhere
I said
but they and he and I
were on Corfu.

Home From The War

Something was always happening at Crewe
When my father came home on The Irish Mail
So that he missed The Princess Maud
And it took him twice as long. Could be
He needed to rest awhile, forget
The jeep rides over deserts, seas of naffi tea,
A common hatred of Montgomery.

Once he sent me a photo of George Formby
And his little dog – both entertained the troops.
My father also played the ukulele. It went well
With his cheery whistling, his matey jokes:
'If the sky fell we'd catch larks.' He sent
His money home, what little he was paid
For fighting Jerry and the Iti Brigade.

'Reported missing, presumed dead',
Best joke of the war for him, home on leave
And drinking tea when the telegram came –
My mother'd had her hair done –
'That's the army for you' he said
But for all I saw of him, he might as well.
Twice he was nearly killed,

In a truck got the speed wobbles –
I couldn't understand how in all that sand
It mattered. And a Red Cross plane
Dropped like a stone before the second engine
At 800 feet, took them out of it,
He strapped to a stretcher with sciatica
And the bronichals, all from the heat.

In Rome the opera still played. He cried
At La Bohéme. And cried to see the children
Without food. Gave up his chocolate ration.
At home my mother cried because the PO
Lost her paybook. She said she couldn't cope.
In 1945 he came home, on a hot day
Went fishing in the river, had a heart attack.

It could have been the Players' cigarettes,
Could have been the canteen gin although
He pleaded war strain. Six medals from the king,
A pension of seventeen shillings a week
For growing up without his family.
When he died at fifty-two it went with him.
My mother went to work to raise a headstone.